BRAIN

PUZZLES FOR KIDS

PICTURE PUZZLES

IN THE WILD

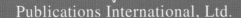

Publications International, Ltd.

Follow us!

@little.grasshopper.books
@publications_international

@PublicationsInternational
@BrainGames.TM

Keep learning! Visit us at:
www.littlegrasshopperbooks.com
www.pilbooks.com

Wonderful Wilderness

Explore jungles, journey across deserts, travel through grasslands, and trek over frozen tundra in this collection of wild picture puzzles. Every puzzle is specially designed for kids to be challenged and entertained. Plus, with 120 puzzles and a wide variety of types and topics, there is something here for everyone.

Each puzzle has a set of directions and answers in the back, so kids can easily work through these alone or play along with an adult. So whether they're going on a road trip, enjoying summer vacation, or filling a quiet winter afternoon, kids will have plenty to enjoy and learn.

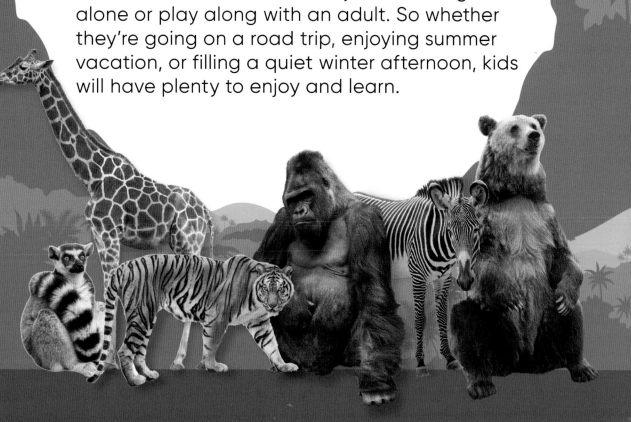

Table of Contents

Finding Foxes

How many foxes do you see? ___6___

Answer on page 139.

In Flight

Find all these things in the picture.

Savanna Animals

Across	Down
3. 	1.
6. 	2. 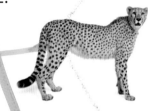
	4. 
	5. 

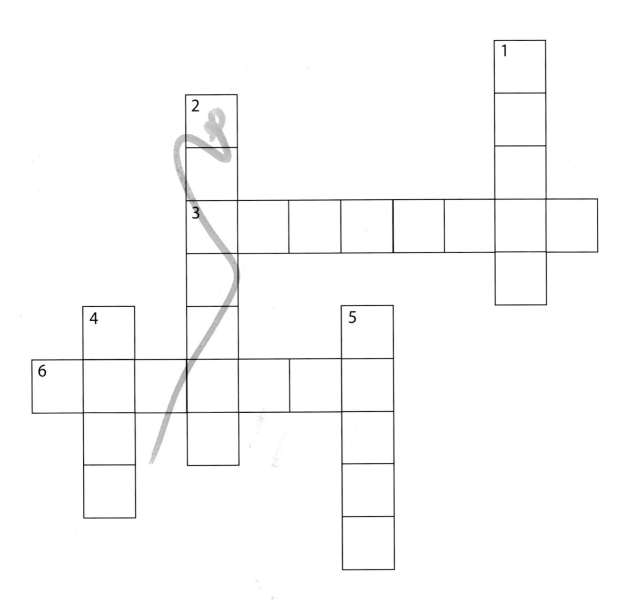

Feathers

Follow the path that goes by all the feathers.
But avoid all the branches!

Start

Finish

Answer on page 139.

Polar Dive

Which piece completes the puzzle?

Ladybugs

Find the 5 differences between these two images.

Answers on page 139.

ALL IN STRIPES

Match each animal to the zoomed-in picture of it.

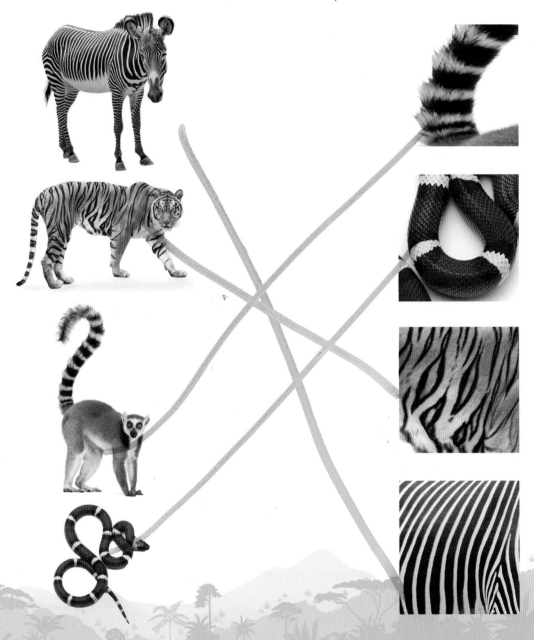

Answers on page 140.

Scrambled Animals

These pictures are all scrambled! Can you tell what each one is?

1.) _ _ _ _ _ _ _

2.) _ _ _ _ _ _ _

3.) _ _ _ _

Answers on page 140.

ALL IN A LINE

- -

Step 1: Look at this picture for one minute.
Remember as much as you can! Then turn the page.

ALL IN A LINE (CONT'D)

Step 2: What is different in this picture?

Answers on page 140.

Which Bears Where?

Match each bear to its twin.

Answers on page 140.

Pick One

Find the one butterfly that:
Has black on the top tips of its wings?
Has orange markings?
Has blue markings?

Answer on page 140.

IN THE TREES

Connect each image to its misssing half.

WITH THE HERD

Find 4 things wrong with this picture.

Answers on page 141.

Flock

Find the two birds that are exactly the same.

BIG CATS

Match each cat to its shadow.

Answers on page 141.

In the Desert

These pictures are all scrambled! Can you tell what each one is?

1.) _ _ _ _ _ _ _ _ _

2.) _ _ _

3.) _ _ _ _ _ _

4.) _ _ _ _ _

Eye See

Which piece completes the puzzle?

Answer on page 141.

Hippity Hoppity

Follow the path that goes by all the green frogs.
But avoid all the yellow frogs!

Start

Finish

Froggy Mystery

Find the one frog that:
Has black spots?
Has orange parts?
Has black eyes?
Has blue parts?

Answer on page 141.

IT'S A PARTY

Step 1: Look at this picture for one minute. Remember as much as you can! Then turn the page.

IT'S A PARTY (CONT'D)

Step 2: What is different in this picture?

Answers on page 142.

Lost in the Herd

Find the two zebras that are exactly the same.

Answers on page 142.

ICY HANGOUT

How many penguins have open mouths? ___
How many penguins are looking down? ___
How many are looking to your right? ___

Answers on page 142.

Twin Tree Frogs

Match each frog to its twin.

Answers on page 142.

Close Up

Which piece completes the puzzle?

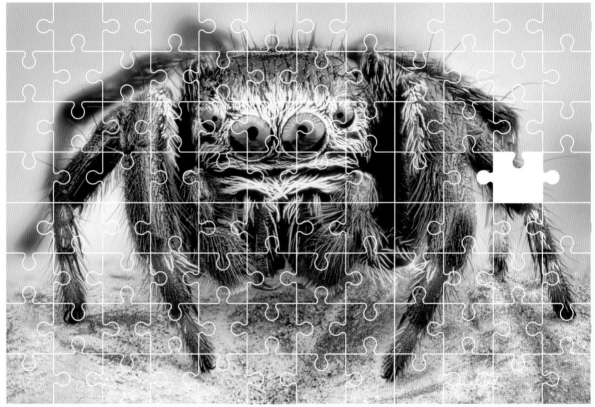

Answer on page 142.

Cut Up

These pictures are all scrambled! Can you tell what each one is?

1.) _ _ _ _ _

2.) _ _ _ _ _ _ _ _ _

3.) _ _ _ _ _

4.) _ _ _ _

Answers on page 142.

Jungle Animals

Across

2.

4.

7.

Down

1.

3.

4.

5.

6.

REFLECTION

What's wrong in this picture?

Answer on page 143.

IN THE SHADOWS

Match each insect to its shadow.

Answers on page 143.

FLYING CLOSE

Match each bird to the zoomed-in picture of it.

Answers on page 143.

In Plain Sight

Find all these things in the picture.

Flower Field

Find the 5 differences between the top and bottom flowers.

40

In the Hot Tub

Which piece completes the puzzle?

Jaguar Pair

Find the two jaguars that are exactly the same.

Answers on page 144.

Birds of a Feather

These pictures are all scrambled! Can you tell what each one is?

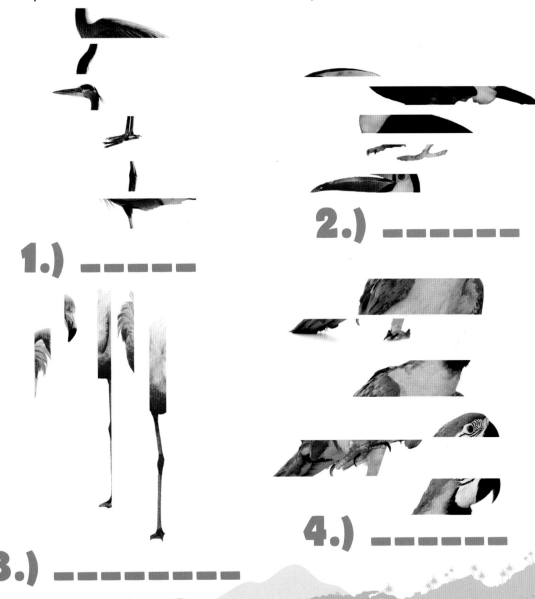

1.) _ _ _ _ _

2.) _ _ _ _ _ _

3.) _ _ _ _ _ _ _ _

4.) _ _ _ _ _ _

ALL TOGETHER

How many animals have antlers?   _____

How many animals have spots?   _____

How many animals have stripes?   _____

Answers on page 144.

Wolf Pack

Match each wolf to its twin.

BRIGHT BIRDS

Match each flamingo to its shadow.

Answers on page 144.

Bug Out!

Follow the path that goes by all the beetles.
But avoid all the butterflies!

Start

Finish

Hunting For Dinner

Find all these things in the picture.

Answers on page 145.

With the Chitals

Find 2 things wrong with this picture.

BUTTERFLY CATCHING

Match each butterfly to the zoomed-in picture of it.

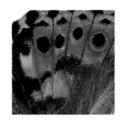

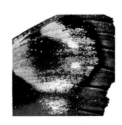

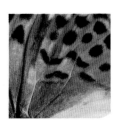

Answers on page 145.

For the Birds

Find the 4 differences between these two images.

Matching Monkeys

Find the two monkeys that are exactly the same.

Answers on page 145.

Follow the Bird

Find the one bird that:
Has not spread its wings?
Has blue markings?
Has red markings?
Has no green on its feathers?

Answer on page 145.

Hopping Along

Match each grasshopper to its twin.

54

Answers on page 146.

Lizards

Follow the path that goes by all the lizards.
But avoid all the snakes!

Start

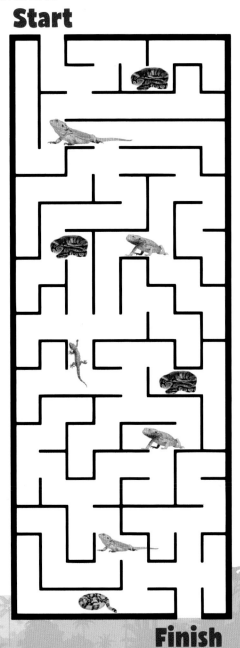

Finish

Answer on page 146.

AUTUMN LEAVES

Connect each image to its missing half.

Answers on page 146.

BUSY BEES

Step 1: Look at this picture for one minute. Remember as much as you can! Then turn the page.

BUSY BEES (CONT'D)

Step 2: What is different in this picture?

Answers on page 146.

Flit and Flutter

Find the 3 differences between these two images.

Answers on page 146.

JOURNEY TO THE SEA

Find 3 things wrong with this picture.

Answers on page 146.

Reach!

Find all these animals in the picture.

SKIN AND SCALES

Match each reptile to the zoomed-in picture of it.

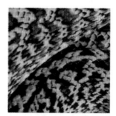

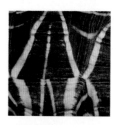

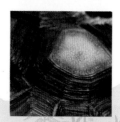

Answers on page 147.

In the Leaves

Match each leaf to its twin.

Flowery

Which piece completes the puzzle?

Answer on page 147.

THE SAVANNA

Step 1: Look at this picture for one minute. Remember as much as you can! Then turn the page.

THE SAVANNA (CONT'D)

Step 2: What is different in this picture?

Answers on page 147.

Hop Along

Find the one bunny that:
Has all four legs on the ground?
Has brown markings?
Holds its head and ears up?
Is looking to the right?

Answer on page 147.

My Shadow and Me

Match each frog to its shadow.

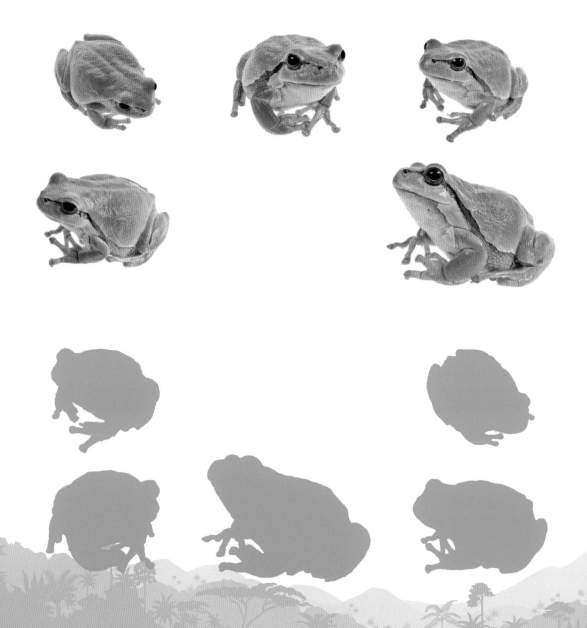

Answers on page 148.

Out at Night

These pictures are all scrambled! Can you tell what each one is?

1.) _ _ _ _ _ _

2.) _ _ _

3.) _ _ _

4.) _ _ _ _

Answers on page 148.

SPOTTED

Match each animal to the zoomed-in picture of it.

Answers on page 148.

Lion Cub

Find the two cubs that are exactly the same.

A Flamingo Flamboyance

Find the 2 differences between these two images.

A Flamingo Flamboyance

Eagle's Nest

Follow the path that goes by all the eagles.
But avoid all the ducks!

74

Answer on page 148.

Hiding

How many deer are hiding in the trees? _____

Find the Rhymes

Find the animal that rhymes with each picture! For example, if the picture shows a pair of socks, the answer might be fox.

Across

1.

3.

4.

5.

6.

7.

Down

2.

3.

4.

WORKING BEES

What's wrong in this picture?

Answer on page 149.

A Conspiracy of Lemurs

Find the one lemur that:
Has white markings?
Has yellow eyes?
Is sitting?
Has gray markings?

Take Flight

Which piece completes the puzzle?

Answer on page 149.

IN THE SHADOWS

Match each bird with its shadow.

Answers on page 149.

Flowers Aplenty

Follow the path that goes by all the pink flowers.
But avoid all the yellow ones!

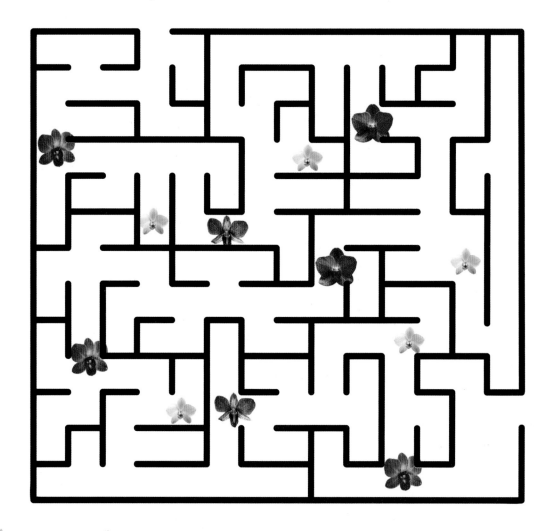

Answer on page 150.

AMPHIBIANS OF PERU

Match each frog or toad to the zoomed-in picture of it.

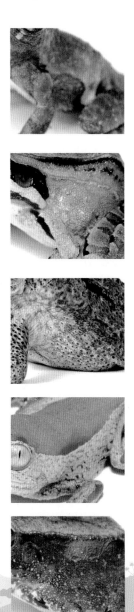

Answers on page 150.

Birds

Across

3.

5.

7.

8.

10.

Down

1.

2.

4.

6.

8.

9.

Feathers

Find the 3 differences between the feathers on top and the ones on bottom.

Answers on page 150.

LOOK AROUND

Step 1: Look at this picture for one minute. Remember as much as you can! Then turn the page.

LOOK AROUND (CONT'D)

Step 2: What is different in this picture?

Answers on page 150.

In the Forest

Match each animal to its shadow.

Answers on page 150.

Field of Flowers

How many pink flowers are there? ____

How many plants have lots of little flowers, instead of one big flower? ____

How many flowers do you see with big yellow centers? ____

Answers on page 151.

Little Kits

Find the two foxes that are exactly the same.

Among the Orchids

Connect each flower to its missing half.

Answers on page 151.

Too Many Bugs

Match each insect to its twin.

Cold Climate Creaturess

These pictures are all scrambled! Can you tell what each one is?

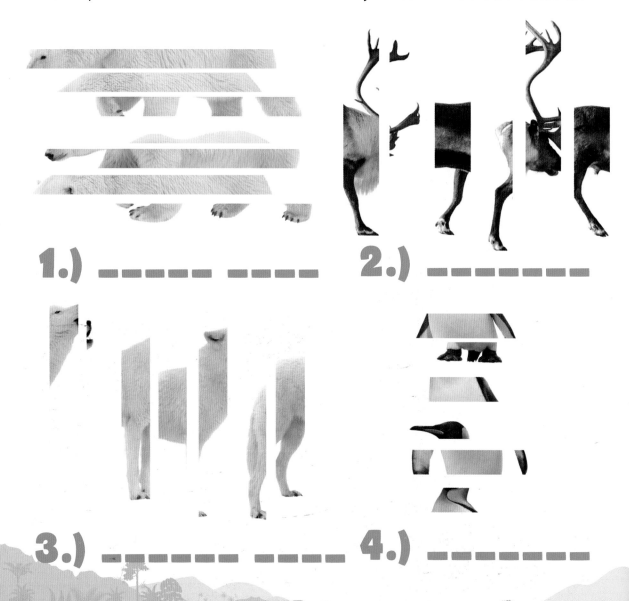

1.) _ _ _ _ _   _ _ _ _

2.) _ _ _ _ _ _ _

3.) _ _ _ _ _ _   _ _ _ _

4.) _ _ _ _ _ _ _

Answers on page 151.

Over the Jungle

Find all these animals in the picture.

Leaf Lunch

Which piece completes the puzzle?

Answer on page 152.

Fluttering Butterflies

Find the two butterflies that are exactly the same.

Lizard Match

Match each lizard to its twin.

Answer on page 152.

CAMOUFLAGE

Where is the caterpillar?

Answer on page 153.

Tiny Animals

These pictures are all scrambled! Can you tell what each one is?

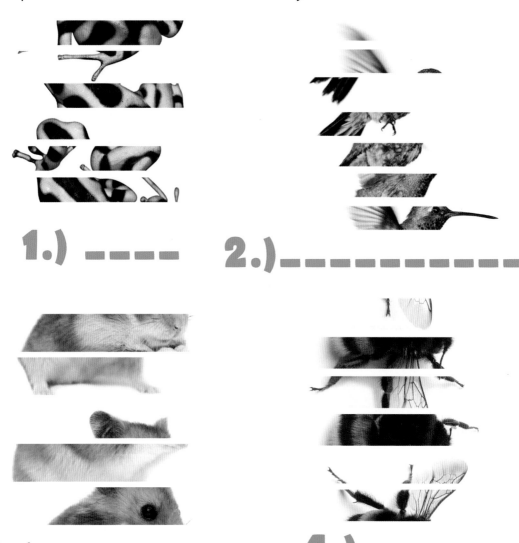

1.) _ _ _ _

2.) _ _ _ _ _ _ _ _ _ _ _ _

3.) _ _ _ _ _ _ _

4.) _ _ _

Answers on page 153.

Bears

Follow the path that goes by all the bears.
But avoid all the trees!

Start

Finish

Buzzing Bees

Find the 4 differences between these two images.

Buzzing Bees

Leap

Find all these animals in the picture.

Answers on page 153.

DREAMY SAFARI

How many vultures are there? _____

What is the biggest animal in the water? _____

Which animal is closest to the giraffe? _____

Answers on page 154.

SOMETHING BLUE

Match each bird to the zoomed-in picture of it.

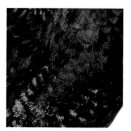

Answers on page 154.

LEAFY PATH

Follow the path that goes by each oak leaf. But avoid the coconuts!

Under the Stars

Which piece completes the puzzle?

Answer on page 154.

Night Flight

Find the 4 differences between these pictures.

Answers on page 154.

Kaleidoscope

Find all these animals in the picture.

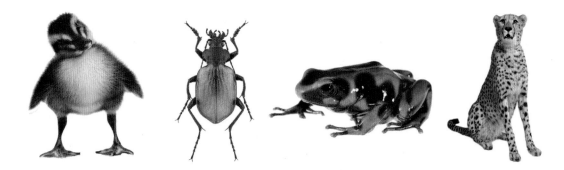

Answers on page 155.

Expert Jumpers

These pictures are all scrambled! Can you tell what each one is?

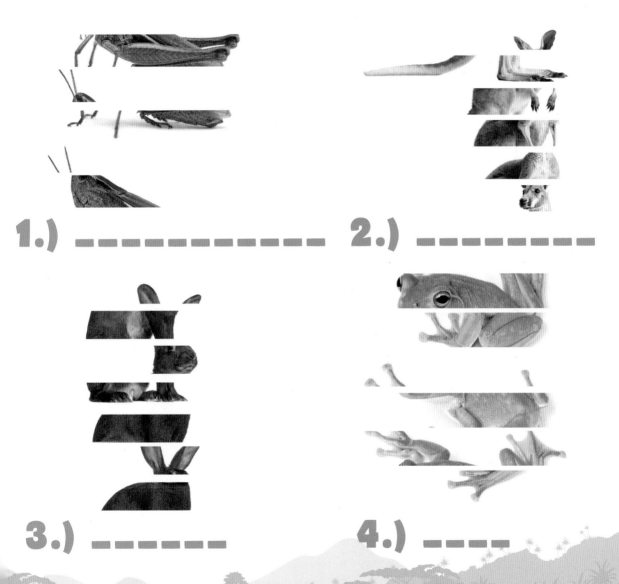

1.) _____

2.) _____

3.) _____

4.) _____

Autumn Colors

- -

Match each tree to its twin.

Answers on page 155.

Baby Birds

Find the one baby bird that:
Has a closed beak?
Has some white markings?
Has feathers on its legs?
Is looking to your right?

Answer on page 155.

Cactus

Match each cactus to its other half.

114

Answers on page 155.

WINTER HERD

Step 1: Look at this picture for one minute. Remember as much as you can! Then turn the page.

WINTER HERD (CONT'D.)

Step 2: What is different in this picture?

Answers on page 156.

POLAR MARCH

What's wrong in this picture?

Answer on page 156.

Birds of Paradise

Find the two flowers that are exactly the same.

Answers on page 156.

LEAFY GREEN

Match each leaf to its shadow.

In the Trees

These pictures are all scrambled! Can you tell what each one is?

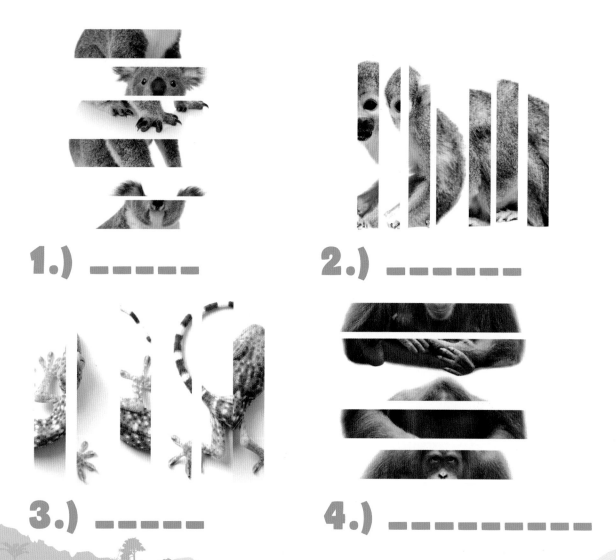

1.) _ _ _ _ _

2.) _ _ _ _ _ _

3.) _ _ _ _ _

4.) _ _ _ _ _ _ _ _ _

Answers on page 157.

Delicate Dance

Which piece completes the puzzle?

Animal Collection

Find the path that goes by all the reptiles. But avoid the mammals!

Start

Finish

Answer on page 157.

Curious Squirrels

Which squirrel:
Is not looking to your right?
Has fewer than four feet touching the ground?
Is not holding anything?
Does not have any white markings that you can see?

Answer on page 157.

Many Moths

Find the two moths that are exactly the same.

Answers on page 157.

In the Cold

Match each arctic wolf to its twin.

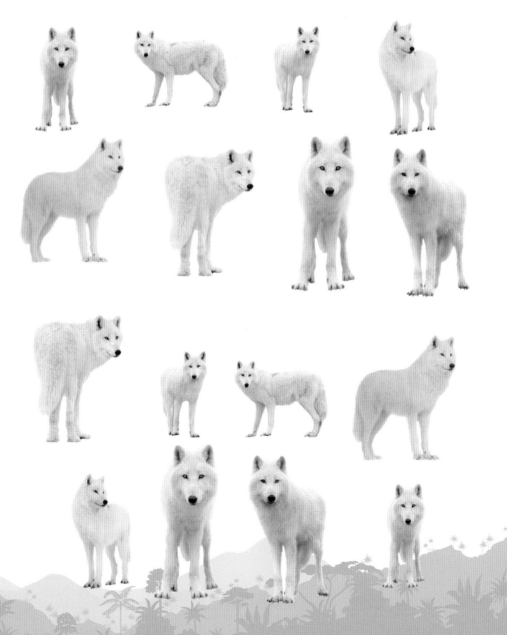

Answers on page 158.

Wild Play

Which piece completes the puzzle?

Answer on page 158.

Slowpokes

These pictures are all scrambled! Can you tell what each one is?

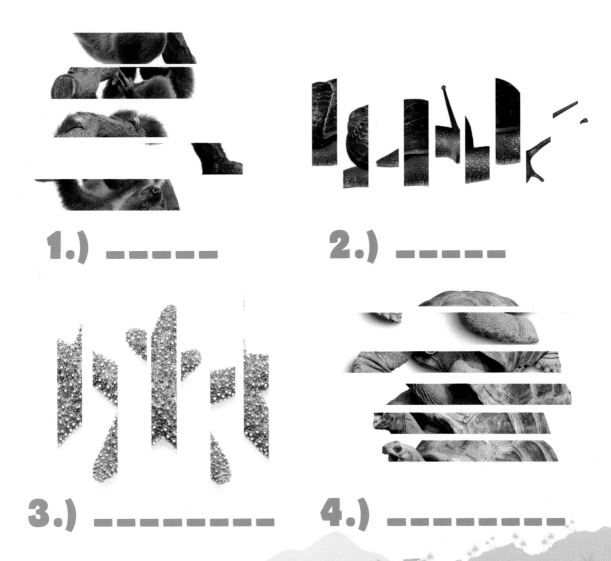

1.) _ _ _ _ _

2.) _ _ _ _ _

3.) _ _ _ _ _ _ _ _

4.) _ _ _ _ _ _ _ _

LAKE VISIT

What's wrong in this picture?

Answers on page 158.

CASTING SHADOWS

Match each frog to its shadow.

BRIGHT AND BOLD

Match each animal to the zoomed-in picture of it.

Answers on page 159.

Hangin' Around

Find each snake in the picture.

In the Fall

Find the 6 differences between these pictures.

Answers on page 159.

In the Dark

Which piece completes the puzzle?

Answer on page 159.

Panda Pals

Find the two pandas that are exactly the same.

134

Answers on page 160.

Speedy

These pictures are all scrambled! Can you tell what each one is?

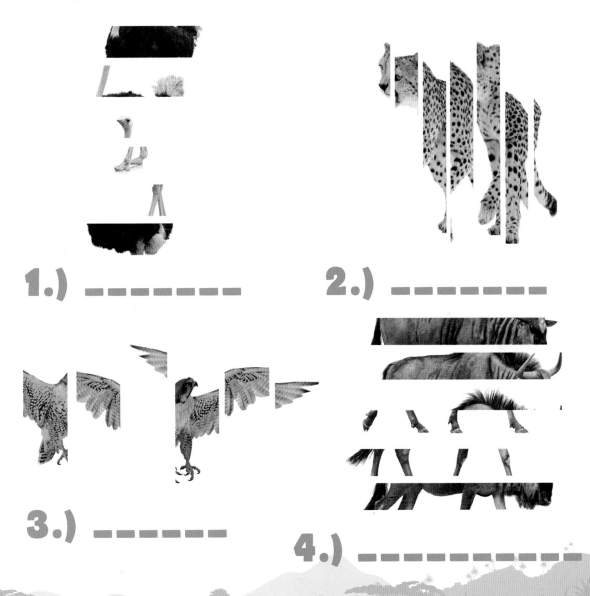

1.) _ _ _ _ _ _ _

2.) _ _ _ _ _ _ _

3.) _ _ _ _ _ _

4.) _ _ _ _ _ _ _ _ _ _

CLIMBING UP

Match each lizard to its shadow.

Answers on page 160.

BABY ANIMALS

Step 1: Look at this picture for one minute. Remember as much as you can! Then turn the page.

BABY ANIMALS (CONT'D.)

Step 2: What is different in this picture?

Answers on page 160.

Finding Foxes (page 6)
There are 6 foxes.

In Flight (page 7)

Savanna Animals (page 9)

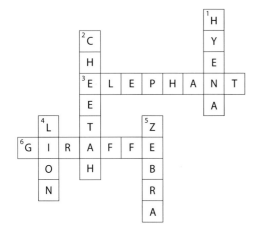

Feathers (page 10)

Polar Dive (page 11)

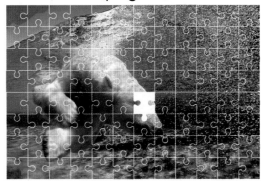

Ladybugs (page 12)

All in Stripes (page 13)

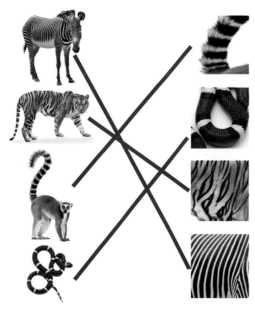

Scrambled Animals (page 14)
1.) Peacock
2.) Giraffe
3.) Wolf

All in a Line (page 15)

Which Bear Where? (page 17)

Pick One (page 18)

In the Trees (page 19)

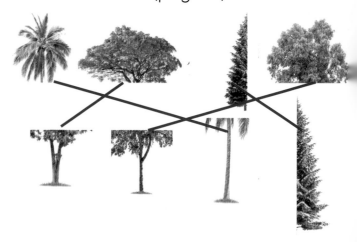

With the Herd (page 20)

Flock (page 21)

Big Cats (page 22)

In the Desert (page 23)
1. Scorpion
2. Fox
3. Spider
4. Snake

Eye See (page 24)

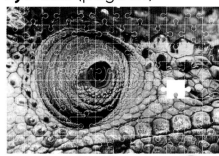

Hippity Hoppity (page 25)

Froggy Mystery (page 26)

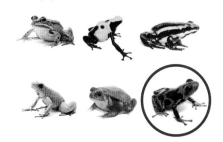

141

It's a Party (page 27)

Lost in the Herd (page 29)

Icy Hangout (page 30)
2, 1, 5

Twin Tree Frogs (page 31)

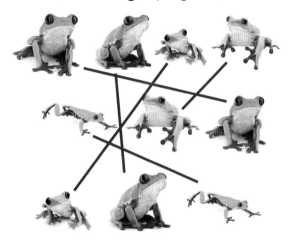

Close Up (page 32)

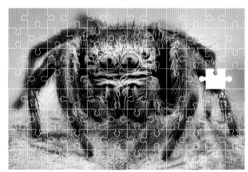

Cut Up (page 33)

1. Rhino
2. Butterfly
3. Eagle
4. Goat

Jungle Animals (page 34)

```
              ¹J
 ²M  A  C  A   W
              G              ³S
     ⁴T  O  U  C  A  N       N
     I        A              A
     G        R              K
    ⁵M  E           ⁶S       E
⁷G  O  R  I  L  L   A
    N              O
    K              T
    E              H
    Y
```

Reflection (page 36)

In the Shadows (page 37)

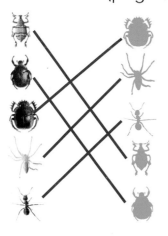

Flying Close (page 38)

In Plain Sight (page 39)

Flower Field (page 40)

In the Hot Tub (page 41)

Jaguar Pair (page 42)

Birds of a Feather (page 43)
1. Crane
2. Toucan
3. Flamingo
4. Parrot

All Together (page 44)
4, 3, 1

Wolf Pack (page 45)

Bright Birds (page 46)

Bug Out! (page 47)

Hunting for Dinner (page 48)

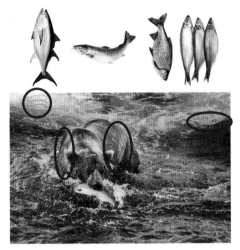

With the Chitals (page 49)

Butterfly Catching (page 50)

For the Birds (page 51)

Matching Monkeys (page 52)

Follow the Bird (page 53)

Hopping Along (page 54)

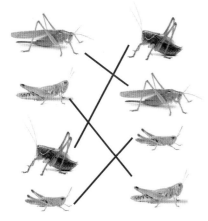

Lizards (page 55)

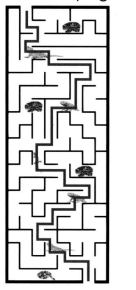

Autumn Leaves (page 56)

Busy Bees (page 57)

Flit and Flutter (page 59)

Journey to the Sea (page 60)

Reach! (page 61)

Skin and Scales (page 62)

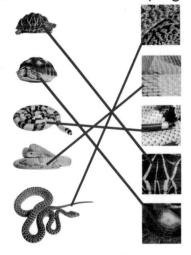

In the Leaves (page 63)

Flowery (page 64)

The Savanna (page 65)

Hop Along (page 67)

My Shadow and Me (page 68)

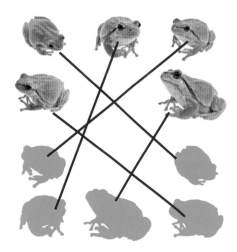

Out at Night (page 69)

1. Racoon
2. Bat
3. Owl
4. Moth

Spotted (page 70)

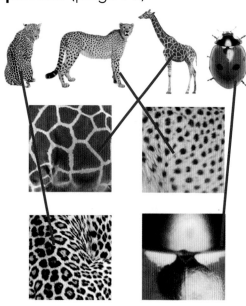

Lion Cub (page 71)

A Flamingo Flamboyance (page 72)

Eagle's Nest (page 74)

Hiding (page 75)
1 deer

Find the Rhymes (page 76)

		¹P	I	²G	
				O	
				A	
		³B	A	T	
⁴M	O	U	S	E	
	O			A	
⁵F	R	O	G		⁶C R A N E
	S				
	⁷H	E	N		

Working Bees (page 78)

A Conspiracy of Lemurs (page 79)

Take Flight (page 80)

In the Shadows (page 81)

Answers

Flowers Aplenty (page 82)

Amphibians of Peru (page 83)

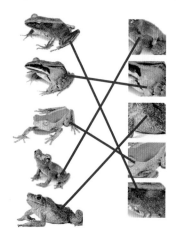

Birds (page 84)

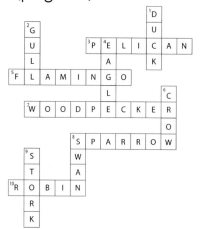

Feathers (page 86)

Look Around (page 87)

In the Forest (page 89)

Field of Flowers (page 90)
2, 2, 6

Too Many Bugs (page 93)

Little Kits (page 91)

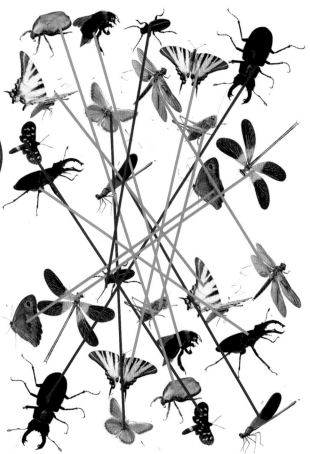

Among the Orchids (page 92)

Cold Climate Creatures
(page 94)
1. Polar Bear
2. Caribou
3. Arctic Wolf
4. Penguin

Over the Jungle (page 95)

Fluttering Butterflies (page 97)

Leaf Lunch (page 96)

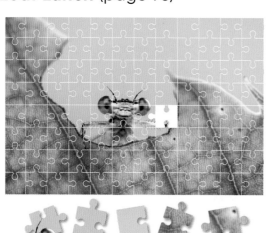

Lizard Match (page 98)

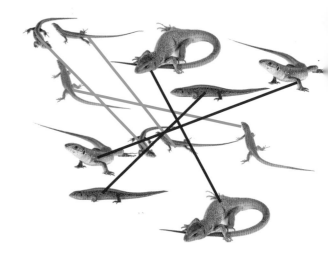

Camouflage (page 99)

Buzzing Bees (page 102)

Tiny Animals (page 100)
1. Frog
2. Hummingbird
3. Hamster
4. Bee

Leap (page 104)

Bears (page 101)

153

Dreamy Safari (page 105)
3, Hippo, Buffalo

Something Blue (page 106)

Leafy Path (page 107)

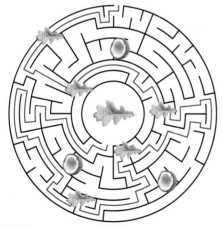

Under the Stars (page 108)

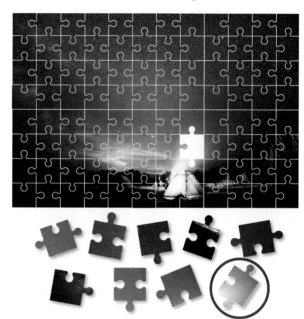

Night Flight (page 109)

Kaleidoscope (page 110)

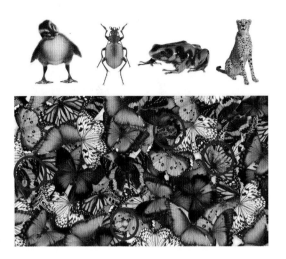

Expert Jumpers (page 111)
1.) Grasshopper
2.) Kangaroo
3.) Rabbit
4.) Frog

Autumn Colors (page 112)

Baby Birds (page 113)

Cactus (page 114)

155

Winter Herd (page 115)

Polar March (page 117)

Birds of Paradise (page 118)

Leafy Green (page 119)

In the Trees (page 120)
1.) Koala
2.) Monkey
3.) Gecko
4.) Orangutan

Delicate Dance (page 121)

Animal Collection (page 122)

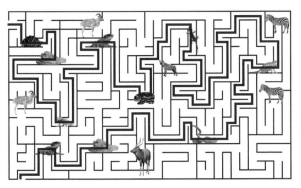

Curious Squirrels (page 123)

Many Moths (page 124)

In the Cold (page 125)

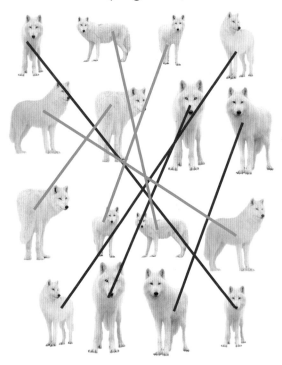

Slowpokes (page 127)

1.) Sloth
2.) Snail
3.) Starfish
4.) Tortoise

Lake Visit (page 126)

Wild Play (page 126)

Casting Shadows (page 129)

Bright and Bold (page 130)

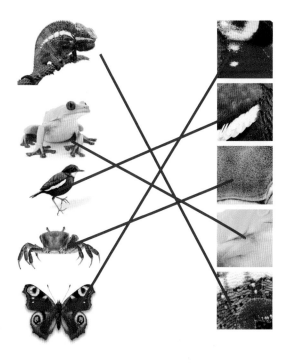

Hangin' Around (page 131)

In the Fall (page 132)

In the Dark (page 133)

Panda Pals (page 134)

Climbing Up (page 136)

Baby Animals (page 137)

Speedy (page 135)
1.) Ostrich
2.) Cheetah
3.) Falcon
4.) Wildebeest